P9-AGN-885

DATE DUE

JUL 0 8

Demco, Inc. 38-293

Give the Body Back

Poems by

Stephanie Strickland

University of Missouri Press

Columbia and London

Library of Congress Cataloging-in-Publication Data

Strickland, Stephanie.
    Give the body back : poems / by Stephanie Strickland.
        p.   cm.
    ISBN 0–8262–0809–6 (alk. paper). — ISBN 0–8262–0810–X (pbk. :
alk. paper)
    I. Title
PS3569.T69543G58   1991
811'.54—dc20   91–25755
                                                    CIP

⊗™This paper meets the minimum requirements of the American
National Standard for Permanence of Paper for Printed Library
Materials, Z39.48, 1984.

Designer: Rhonda Gibson
Typesetter: Connell-Zeko Type & Graphics
Printer: Thomson-Shore, Inc.
Binder: Thomson-Shore, Inc.
Typeface: Elante

For Mary King Mellon
  Ruth Margaret Voigt
  Robin Wallace Strickland Pfaff

Contents

Acknowledgments

I wish to express thanks to Yaddo, the MacDowell Colony, the Ragdale Foundation, the New York State Creative Artists Public Service (CAPS) program, and the National Endowment for the Arts for awards that supported this work.

Grateful acknowledgment is made to the following publications, in which these poems, or earlier versions of them, first appeared: "First Couple" and "Mother: Dressed Up," *Agni Review*; "The Subject: Girl, by Vermeer" (as "Girl, by Vermeer"), *Chowder Review*; "Lives of the Saints," *Columbia: A Magazine of Poetry & Prose*; "The Artistry Of Girls: Poem for Nabokov, Carroll, Cornell" (as "Poem for Nabokov, Carroll, Cornell"), *Croton Review*; "How We Love Now," "Love That Gives Us Ourselves," and "When I Get There," *Iowa Review*; "At Sea: For an Old Haitian Woman" (as "For an Old Haitian Woman"), "From the New World," and "Hospital," *Ironwood*; "Milk in Glass Bottles," *Kenyon Review*; "End of the Night," *Little Magazine*; "Sweat," *New Virginia Review*; "Negative," *Pequod*; "Consort" and "Living on Air," *Ploughshares*; "Leaving," *Poetry Now*; "The Mute" (as "Harder"), *Porch*; "Shadow," "She Doesn't Care," and "Use of Icons," *Prairie Schooner*; "Nasturtium," *Slant*; "My Mother's Body," *Soundings East*; "Visiting the Woods" (as "Visitor"), *Southern Poetry Review*; "In April" and "Seeing a Medusa," *Tendril*; "Exposure," "Listing," "The Old Woman Said," and "The Oldest Inside," *West Branch*.

Several of these poems have also appeared in a chapbook, *Beyond This Silence* (State Street Press).

Give the Body Back

Seeing a Medusa

Only that tinge of crimson-pink
like cyclamen flashing
drew me down, made me see you

in the heave of the wake, all
pale-jelly innard
on your side, resisting nothing

in the wash of green glass, clear gray, the waves
calm today, steady, as you slap
up and down in their hands: a nest

of tentacles rolling with the foam,
then hanging, white with poison. You collapse
an inbreath of water, shudder. Glide.

Gone, before I grew faint
leaning over the boat; gone,
before I even knew

it was you—alive! Not knowing. Reliving
the blow, remembering: you, torn out, despised,
and flung dripping to the waves.

Exposure

What she said. Something mild. Some opinion.
I was a child: all I heard, all I remember,
her eyes, when his whipsaw turn, his rising shoulders
told her, she shouldn't have spoken—

A memory I carry heavily. Over and over
in this underground river of memories I can't see,
I inch against the current, remembering
a grotto, searing my lungs to bring something: is it

something, Mother, these handfuls
of seaweed, wet, clinging, iodine-rich? As she is,
so thin, holding them from her, she goes at once
from rock to rock, in dark lenses,

white linen, spreading them in the sun.
It takes my breath away, how soon they dry—
She is asking if everyone is well.
I am answering. Fine. They are fine.

Sweat

If I laugh louder now, unfrightened,
dream dreams to their conclusion,
the face of my mother as a young woman
close to my face, both of us, two of us
wrestling closer and closer on a bed,

if I don't stop the dream, if I don't let
the seizures wake me completely
—these are people I know, whose faces
I know: my husband, dreamed,
who sleeps at my breast, restless,

if I am less afraid
of what I lose—of the connection
I am to all I lose; if I care less
that I'm cruel, marked
by my father's grit, his invitation;

if I dream of blood, of Hathor's rage
appeased by a deception, the field soaked
with red beer, of Isis as a falcon
ravishing the corpse, and laugh aloud
touching men and women; if I tire of this

and sleep, and if my mother,
a young woman, grips me so tight
with her arms and legs that I am filled
with torment, with a kind of light
which makes me speak

in the dream, say *I love you so*;
later sweat with this blessing,
think, where are you now?
Have you come to me now?
It is not too late.

First Couple

Startle-fright
when you jump me.
Swaddled panic when
you cut me off, tenderly
pin me to your breast,
the bed, a table.
I can smell
something coming,
but I fail here, submit
to your intent eyeing,
your conspiracy of whispers,
butterfly kisses, Eskimo,
leopard. Assiduous
mother, anticipating
any move: your eyes,
all the same, mild, blue,
alive now—only now—
pursuing me, your baby,
your newborn,
your cripple, whose whole
body gazes up at you
and trembles.

She Doesn't Care

She doesn't care—she says. Her coat
is loose, she's glassy-eyed: the girl's
lips are blue; long since, bluish-gray.

Stiffer, more dogged than the rest,
she breasts the hill churning
with sleds, dodging runners, pushing forward

to the top of the ledge rock, elbowing in,
making room to take off. She hesitates,
sighting the run, but doesn't

pull back from the brink; instead, throws
her sled to the ground and slams down on it.
Now the sun has set, the track is dull, slick,

a sheet of glimmer toward the low wall
at the end. Not like this. On her belly.
To go without stopping,

without thinking: Get up! she tells
herself, and stands, again, dazed.
Then, as she has done all day, wooden slats

gripped to her ribs, she runs and leaps out
from the edge. Her eyes are shut;
she's going blind, headlong

for the joy, the pounding as the first
arc-rise sinks beneath her and keeps sinking
faster; coldness and cold

wind, increasing. More. Faster. She is sure
this is joy, the terror she feels
in her body hurtling down.

Amphibian

All day I think of that frog
made to lie open, to empty
convulsively.

All day I limp; I feel
like crying. It's not
just you, or how you use your strength—

It's that time
they injected her with hormones
to make her give birth

in class: the instructor
squeezing
eggs out of her, over and over,

like stripping milk
from a teat; shaking out
the last drops. I got sick.

When I came back, the body:
dropped in a sink—
breathing.

This morning
in the dark, prolonged, split
second, as I wanted to get up

but began to know, you didn't, a flash—
the stone house in Italy,
all gray tones

and blurred—a photograph,
from a physics textbook:
Volta, in his garden. On something

like a doll's clothesline,
just a string really, are
the frogs hanging, and the legs of frogs.

Consort

And what did that make her?
Forcing him to do it. She didn't like
insistence, only because she could never pace

or gauge it—faster: his panic burning off, buried
in her pores like mist. No distance; skin,
whose it was, whose limb even, unclear.

She didn't like binding him,
full of being bound. She liked amnesia:
each day to discover another

sun, sinking on both, for both the same,
almost; more gold on his face
and fishhook grin, more solar pressure on her hip

when she limped. She liked
no cog, no evident intent, no emotion at all—
except surprise: the cooled orange of carrots torn

into strange air, circles of greenlight
feathering, enfolding them, lifted away:
holes in the ground

redug toward water, and deeper, toward garnet needles
bursting their matrix, spike after spike
like Viking boats,

like stars
in an Arctic night. And darker still, wider,
still exactly what she was.

The Artistry of Girls: Poem for Nabokov, Carroll, Cornell

I, too, am brutal. My eyes move like knives
in your filigree forests. Hedges
don't stop me, nor intricate thickets: what
I can cut through, I am content with; it's

the figure in the clearing I resist. You see
she moved me, the way you displayed her, paper
flat, in cerulean depth: a maiden in ermine,
in doily, in Valentine candy box lace.

Little skater, little baby shoe, Goldilocked girlchild,
flushed, with hectic cheeks: I traded my soul
for your twelve- your seven- your four-year-old
seductiveness; I made my child like you, elfin, cherubic.

My hands, too, hide in a white muff. I think I am
this baby innocent. I'm not: I'm the mother giving
suck to the Sweet Tooth whose mouth drains
my nipple. Such equivocal pain, isn't it Joseph?

Vladimir? Lewis? No. Not the same. You mount
the specimen, fix the glass. You see
it's different for me. I'm in here. I wait
with an eager smile, my body my alias.

My Mother's Body

Little by little, exhausting her: frightened body
waves of nausea are hollowing.
Moved through
like a dune, become the sweep
of a palm through sand, my mother's body
became like sand, breached, a memory
of outline. Her lungs
fill with water, a hull overturned, sails
filling with water, toss, stiffen
in the sunlight. Again
submerge.
Breath at long intervals. Needle-flow
of bubbles in the respirator.
Pure oxygen
forced through her mouth, drying
her lips. "Look,
I've brought gloss. Pomade. I know—
you don't want
smell. No, this has no scent,
no color."
Only her eyebrows.
"Don't wash off my eyebrows,"
she says. They are like wings
of soft brown powder that go nowhere, stopped
at the arch in flight.
This room
crowds her so, even
its light. I push back the flowers.
She loves my father.
She opens
her arms as if the tubes and bandages and wires
were Titania's cape in the moonlight.
"Tell me about writing. . . ."
But
I could not tell her.

Daughter, Twelve

My eyes stroke the glint in your hair,
the fuzz at your temples.
You stand at the window,

staring down the black fret of branches.
Sun, on the snowdrift, bursts
in your face. You turn back to me,

a smile spiraling your whole
body as your arms clasp
overhead. You have guessed

everything: power, desire; everything
but this, how the fire, kindled,
will burn a path between us.

The Old Woman Said

"You think I'm too old
to know what it is?
I know it better than my life.
Don't tell your grandmother how
to suck eggs, Miss. Don't murmur me
desire—a stigma, a block
and not natural," she said, "not
natural enough,
but what they don't teach it,
throw it in your eyes. Look here
child, it's no mean trick
staying alive
in those shells of desire.
Look at your mother's
mission: bleed to feel. 'If
she so *chooses*.'
They put that in, but the truth
of it is, no one refuses,
no one and nothing not part
of the terror
driving that bargain: I make,
you eat—child, there's teeth
in every mouth that waters. You've got
to watch out
for the din of the women, moaning
'Take care, only one thing they want,'
that you don't lose your nerve.
The lie about love
is that it isn't here.
You can feel desire.
Desire is a rouge dress
glowing in the dark. Or it doesn't
glow—but it never comes off:
an oil to conform,
or a chain to control,

the body. The body, child,
is a soul, injured at birth
by people's talk.
It's a shock how harsh, ugly
sometimes, the acts of love
can look. And child, they're not,
ever, what you expect
or want;
because they leave nothing
to language, no more than a drop
shining on a sieve. You
will know them:
they give the body back."

Milk in Glass Bottles

Upright, not incurving bottles, bottles with cream
on the crimped silver cap: what my mother found
in the milk box, built by my dad.

What my mother, then, when someone came,
was so good at was greeting the stranger;
the rhythmic deliverer who came, she prepared for.

It was settled wealth and rhythm: to this day
a clean floor with sunlight on it moves me,
seals me up in some lifted shining cup and I pour

through ample glasses with facets and sunbeams
and Peter Rabbit and Flopsy, lore, on ware
that Wedgewood wanted so badly to spread

to the middle classes. And did. No one comes
anymore. Everyone is here. With us already,
in rerun, with Dolby on chromium tape. Here

on Columbian crystals for vividness: chocolate,
cocoa, coffee, cocaine—and silver, black grains of it,
swirled by the dream czar, sealed in his chamber, his darkroom

under redlight: here on our screen flickering phantoms
reliving as us. The bottles, the window grid,
imposed—not a tax on glass anymore,

but obstacles, to open, to polish: they had
a texture. No double pane
could conceal itself. This action they gave to give

a simulacrum of clearness: full,
or half. Or enough for breakfast. Now, in waxed
paper with lost, have-you-seen-me faces, faces

homogenous, now, in the buses, across
races and genders and eminent
criminals and gas bills. *Have you seen me?*

No. It's not vivid enough, in the grain
of the gray plastic gallon. Everyone,
my son, says we have control, remote, over timing

—order—of image. At first,
I thought the images were various,
abundant, like the Fox Creek Market in Michigan:

berries from black to boysen to blue to logan
to palest gold-juice goose-green staining red
the wooden boxes open to the flies, my finger;

like the Mall Emporium
promised to be. And keeps promising. My son rents
visitors—as videos. We, I mean women

and children, with milk and berries for supper
in our warren, we would wait; someone,
always a stranger, came: "My name is Suzanne—

my Grandmother and I are Bible students."
"Will you sign?" and "What have you girls done
with yourselves today?" The strain of the ones

who came to stay—if they would. It's the grain
that hurts my eyes now; looking closer, I see only
blood and blue phosphors fading green

on the snow-scratched, darkening screen. Then silence.
Her sound. Not now—when she came then, coming
to me around the corners, the covers, who came, who cleaned,

who embraced us. *Don't do this,* she told me,
over spilt milk. It is all, all
spilt. Don't speak of it. Don't, speak. . . .

Lives of the Saints

1

Into the ladlings of sunlight
a gauze curtain dips
its white sieve, brims with yellow, spills
some
and rides wider, emptying.

2

Hidden between bright parsley in a tipped
pot and a crook of gold
squash, the dark
tomato reddens on a white enamel sill
until its shoulders open.

3

Deep scratches web
the blue counter, which is cleared,
cool, and so quiet,
even the spider
stops climbing, hangs in the air.

Nasturtium

Tell me why, then,
I have a hunger as specific
as a pregnant woman's
for parsley or nasturtium leaves.

Tell me why this hunger
is for you—
why it stays in my belly
and won't come to my mouth.

Tell me you know I'm dizzy
briefly, in a room
until I know if you're there;
tell me why we laugh

and how your smile
came to be
that much quicker
than your eyes.

Tell me you're more kind,
more quiet than I think
in your other life,
and why we laugh

happy to be nothing
—and why this hurts.

How We Love Now

In bed you think of her
hollow cheek and strong jaw.
How difficult to graft them
to my apple face. Easier for eyes

than fingers, but your fingers
only go one place,
urge me: you are anxious
to make us disappear on these sheets.

Her silence, her secrets—her complex
attention: how difficult
to graft them to me, who want you,
or not; in season. When I warm

along your length, when our heads touch,
some whole circuit comes complete:
you could be a tree, I rock so high
on a treetop. You are here

for the tree—as I am here for her;
and she reminds you of your mother
when young, a flirt, hardheaded.
The image that compels you

when her long body swings by, you press
to my body, hot, rushing. I am surprised.
I feel her closer to me, now,
than I was ever able to bring her

before. I see how we are using her,
how she has used. And it all comes back,
what that was, being an embodiment; so
matched, to my lover's dream. Leaving him.

You, there. I blamed myself. If only
I weren't restless, I wouldn't have
resisted being exact, the matchless
match. How did we go on then?

This hot afternoon, years later,
when you bring her to my bed,
agitated, I'm remembering him
and what in all this time has stayed unsaid,

how more than once you saved my life,
how many years it took
to say goodbye, to know I'd left;
how I've loved you and with whom.

Listening to Tapes: Bessie Smith

To remember the bruises.
To recognize rooms
I was pushed in.
And stayed there.

Bessie behind me.
Bessie, whose voice
I put on when I want her, letting her
do this work, shift,
carry. Shout.
And grieve. If she instead
had turned on her accusers
—or to someone,
another woman, who would stand for her and say
Enough! Enough! If Bessie herself
had hardened her voice, but how? And I don't
wish for this, I fear it,
the river of her voice running colder and clear.

Her throat, singing
man after man who could make
her do anything
—she said.

I listen
and weep for her sharp
pleasure; for rooms I will return to,
the child I destroyed there;
ongoing harm
I do my daughter.

Listing

Listing with sweetness that rises
inside, spilling over
all around our bodies, so closed,

so stranded in happiness,
we never call to the rose and blue
children floating like cows overhead;

you sink to sleep, an empty hull,
beached on the block of my pelvic bones;
dreaming the sweetness,

tongues like moons on my eyelids.

The Oldest Inside

It *is* simple. Bring me
off any way
at all and I lie quiet,
solved,
beside you. Only, if suddenly
you stumble, some impossible
grief, hunger,
hatred of play in your eyes,
I look away,
I say,
this is make-believe,
this is skill;
but a hole
opens
down
the oldest inside
of my body:
trouble
that can't
be
quieted by you,
by two,
by me.

The Room She Darkened

In the room she darkened against summer,
against sand, and snakes
sunning on the doorstep; the inner room

she dimmed and hushed, in the raw heat,
a burrow of coolness, bounded by
soft air, easy to breach, I was blind

when I burst in, zigzags and sun rings
jagging my eyes; then a blur,
then she, bending over soap and water,

making hoops flutter in a bowl
chipped blue: bubbles we loved blurbling
in rushes, or blown slowly, half-bubbled,

a cluster. I wanted ones that clung
and hung down, they grew so full—and those
that floated, their long, shining

solos deceptive. What could it mean
to be unbroken—like my father?
Our pleasure came from their grace

and the certainty of gravity,
defeat. They carried our breath:
we expanded with each. Swift

shoots of color closed and opened in
their skin, as they turned; I watched them
touch and break. They hurt my mother

some way. She would sadden
past all measure, watching them
break. Breaking them herself.

At Sea: For an Old Haitian Woman

It will float now she thinks;
she has hollowed it
enough. Numbness spreads in
her shoulder, her swollen wrist,
arms lying on the rocker.
Oil lamp in the rafters.
Feet bare on the dirt floor.
She does not remember,
anymore, what is undone—only
the boat, blued with indigo,
brilliant. Single lamp
in the rafters. Blue with indigo
her fingers. He is brilliant, pine
silver, perfect husband, sea-
husband, ready strength, swirling
peace. . . . Dozing, starts up
to shake her rattle; flames
tatter above her in the open hut.
On the swept floor, pillows
with lace, conch shells, roses.
In a night filled with sounds,
the sound of her fan, falling
on her lap. Imperceptibly
rocking, all alone, guarding
the bed. Perfect husband,
sea-husband, who, if he comes,
comes and goes with a roar mild
as mist, in the grizzled
light, mild as any morning
mist, in the first light,
when she finally sleeps,
when the rocker is stopped.

Negative

Hold it up to the light.
It fills with whiteness: the elm, the embrace.
Retrace. You can't. There is blight
and canker. See,
in that candid shot, how all poses.

Cool, once, your eyes.
Whether or not their laggard cry, their after-cry rises,
your heart is helpless, struggling
to close
and like a womb, be competent;

like a womb, refuse.
Flights in the darkness, silver
and green: drive them away. Let the heart burn,
let it burn undisturbed; let it go out
in the resinous night.

Shadow

Vaporized
with no trace.
Relieved of anything
perceptible to bury
or cremate: a broken
cistern of photons,
waves like grain
moving.

The monument:
a gray stain fused
in concrete, a shadow
cast on three steps in Nagasaki
for a moment, by the silvery flash
of the explosion;
etched there by light
from the suns
that exposed it. Not a man.

Not a woman. An effigy: human
by deduction,
like a cloak.

I try to touch
a dark blotch on the screen
the commentators' talk
flows over. Feeling
my mind refuse
invasion, re-fuse
stain, stiffen against
shadowy webs
of the world and its end;

abiding them
in the silo of my body
—there is no other place—
until they are born,
gray, and can dismantle
the silos, shining
by their thousands
on the earth.

Love That Gives Us Ourselves: Muriel Rukeyser

She said disowning
is the only treason. She said we pretend
coldness, or pretend
we are used to the world.
She said
all I touch has failed,
and the beginning was real.
She said, by imagining
the child can cope with loss,
be at home.
It is a work of images, difficult
and bare. Very slow. Like falling in love,
desire shadows its fulfillment.
She said
now I speak only words I can believe,
no sly resonant pity.
Her short questions, the gravel
of her answers comes back to me again
and again, in waves:
turn with your whole life choosing.
Everything here is real, she said,
and of our joy. Her mother
didn't answer. Even past death
language incomplete
between them. Intense
desire scorches its fulfillment.

Mother: Dressed Up

A veil's tiny
black diamonds touch
your lashes, your cheeks.

Perfume ringing
from your wrist, you lean
sideways

on the stair;
your brim, your lips just
brush me.

Faraway,
mild, your eyes
lift to him:

I am stunned
by your body, trying
to hide

its eagerness
to pull away
from mine.

Hospital

An animal,
cradled in your collarbone,
eating.

I rub oil on your feet
and your calves,
lay my cold hands on the wave
of heat in your head.

What hurts you most
is that I stay
and watch it,
watch it lift you in its mouth.
I keep talking, keep stroking.

2

Thoughts settle on her eyes
and sink. Like a candle flame
when the wind stops, her whisper
fills with lucidness. Then gutters.
Nodding deeper, she wonders
why faces roll by like seaweed,
why what is sharper than broken glass
in her mind stays so still, why
the others don't speak of it.

3

A mask of blue veins,
the slow waver of your eyelids

opening on me. The bones
of your fingers and your diamond
cut my hand
as you whisper, *list*. I don't
understand— Your eyes close, *list*.
Yes, I say, I will. I will. I'll do it.
List. I say list . . . list. . . .

The Mute

It's harder than you think
hearing voices, of pins, of crabs.
Under the cut cane of silence,

in the stumps, the char, unclench
your hand: the night
is a pulverized sound,

inner numbers of the world
dropping like counterweights,
old spores; listen . . .

shriveled, black, lost yes,
but that upgush of blood
pushed against a void;

if all you do is look,
you will despise
the broken throat;

you will see the rabbit's tears
as needle tracks
on the fur of its face.

Visiting the Woods

I hate the tall pines down,
their dark green arms curved
over the snow. They look like
mothers in a storm, bodies
thrown completely on the young:
broken limbs, stumps, strips of bark—

this withered, jagged wood
is beautiful: trees rubbed gray,
or silver, if thin; leaves
that curl like parchment
on a dry stem, beds of rusted
needle; the pond, frozen hard.

At the edge of a large field
where at night the stars stand in rivers
of smaller stars, filling
the low sky coming down, closer
to the boulders, a small fire
smokes in a grove. The air, today,

not nearly so freezing: the man
who built the fire leans, unmoving,
on his shovel. We watch the red
transparent movements filling with air,
smell the pine burning.
"Is it all right?"

I ask. "Yes," he said. Then,
very unlike him, he smiled
and said it again: "Yes."

Leaving

A-cree! A-cree! The jay is screeching.
Rain-beaten stems lie flat.
A late wasp burns the fallen apple.

Scraggles of catkin blow in yellow boats
of ash leaves—looseness in our lives
leaves bruises, walls

that were a garden. Not to see you
again. The gate rusts open
in my hand.

Use of Icons

After the mother died,
no one wanted
her rosary of black seeds.

It hangs on my wall
beside a page from the Qur'an
—and two woodcuts: in one,

a stolid vase, a black bottle
with carnations, ruffs
of teeth. But in the other,

this bottle made transparent,
filled with water
by a chisel:

block face cut,
so they can be seen, knuckled
stems of three carnations.

Kneaded through my hands, told
and retold,
knots don't dissolve;

I can't untie them.
For every prayer begun, bottle
flung against the sea,

there is a deeper one,
abandoned,
broken by words

that rise unwanted: faithless, then.
But stung
to prayer: protect her;

instruct him.
Give her pleasures, unmediated, cool
as unguents. Help her stand.

Or is it You
who crush? That fear
roots my silence—

Your silence,
annulling me so long,
left a quiet knife in my side.

I have drawn it out.
It is part of my arm.

In April

Stones hit the glass like gunshot,
sheets of rain run up my windshield in ridges of ice,
hail, forcing branches down,

at the same time mist rises
Could we have stopped you?
from warm ground near the parkway.

As it rises in Rome,
through the Borghese at dawn, a caul of silver
holding the trees like blue-green spears,

exposing the bodies
of young men. Not flaunted, now;
boys—going home. Blossoms, smashed

against the car, the curb, flood the pool
that widens from the sewer. Dogwood. Forsythia.
Why? John?

Your brothers are silent. As they were. I too
say nothing. I leave your death
unopened. Alone. This year

I left a fetus, with so little mention
the surgeon's knife
still feels cold

between my legs. I left a woman
whose sobbing, swollen
face I deny.

She skids in my body.
The way the car
went wild when you pulled.

The Afternoon: Van Gogh

All afternoon, there were
only slurs of light,
too faint to warm the hard
pears in the window.

Steady gray,
growing almost boundless,
squeezed against the clock,
against the pigments:

you stood motionless,
as it climbed your neck
and made the sound
of a shell near your ear.

Around you, now, shadow;
a lamp, pale, in the last of day,
deepens into gold,
into ochre. Corners relent.

The railing leans at peace.
You reach your fingers
into the circle
of decanting light;

your last afternoon.
Tomorrow, in the field,
you will strap your hands
to noon itself.

The Subject: Girl, by Vermeer

Light, bending from bevels
in the leaded casement over her,
amber, pale green, reaches
to the white wall:
it doesn't catch the downcast
eyes beneath her cap.
Leaning forward a little, she might
be dreaming
or holding her breath—
more like acquiescing
to a memory
of pain: one arm outstretched, as if
she'd opened the window
those few inches; the other
lower, fingers cupped
on the handle of a jug, long ago
set down. Lost,
you think. Unaware of her hand
on the pitcher. So stilled,
it's as if that quick
flutter in the silver
were a dove and would fly up,
should she stir; as if
she knows she can outwait
pain. Or does she look
for someone to come
—to reappear? No fear,
no yearning, show
in her face. Her forearms
and wrists, free of the heavy
yellow sleeves, disappear in strips
of shadow and sunlight. The iron
rod, steadying
a wall map, points its finial
directly at her neck, to focus

her there. It holds her:
it forestalls.
Intently quiet,
listening lightly for something
to skim past—
or is she repeating
a spell she is weaving
of the moment before
she was taken? She is young,
young enough to imagine
that if she doesn't waver, no
fall will occur;
it will all be there,
unharmed, when Vermeer
releases her
slowly, from his gaze.

End of the Night

Walking with you
the darkest margin;
reaches of dimness

above us are blue, first blue
—a hover. Mother,
remember, the black

bass in the bay black
with black sand?
A down feather strays

against the coarse cloth
of your apron,
your twisting hands.

If I were air
and could touch you,
like air. Cool before sunrise.

Black blossoms cluster
at your feet on a gray vine,
the blue field curving. Don't

give way—to bewilderment,
their laughter.
Even when the sun shatters

forth, as it will, and soaks you
with glitter, a cellar
is dark. Ice, too,

hidden in the earth,
lined with blue.
I would erase for you,

undo it all,
if I could. Keep them,
in the rough crib: stubs of blue

pencil, blue quinces,
blue barns. First
blue

at the end of the night
—it is you.
Not the child.

From the New World

More vivid, even,

        than the Morpho,
  more still than the Sphinx moth,
    oar-winged,
      warlike,
    you attack and drive off hawks.

    No pigment—only light,
        split
          through rigid
structures in your barbules
into ribbons:
       crimson,
    ruby,
fire-green.

Grackles, gouramis, peacocks, scarabs:
        your foils.
None
   so radiant so swift: your colors
  never strut
  never shift in display.
     They are there.
    Are not.
       And again.
   And again
   not.

We
      are huge. We hang back. We can feel your hum
             on our horizon,
    see a furious
blur out there in the garden this morning
near the vine.

       Torpid,
       by night;
             flushed with blue
                  skylight, your heart, the discs
                     of your wings
                            spin,

             scatter

cinders of quickness;

  burning their fuel,
not to soar,
           to stand still
               over the flower;
          shaking so little

     the needle

   bill and tubular tongue
that touch the dark
     throat of the blossom.

Living on Air

1

Exact and tyrannical
intelligence in women: in their bodies. Not ventriloquy,
acumen: the splintered eye refusing
a caduceus, a tree-of-life, or any surface wholeness
to swirl beakers of light. Bodies of women
constructing two solutions from the same vinegared
mother, whose uncleaving polarizes light: black,
or bright, a light that can't pass till it's twisted.
Discovered in acid
crystals of new wine by an indifferent eye. Hard
and indifferent. Like the body of a woman
defenseless with what it knows, feeling this happen
too many times. My sinister hand
unlike the right one, now; and my greenhouse
not a solarium. The cockatoo has gone
and in its place a raven crazed
by lighted space.

2

Unlike myself, in the secret divisions
which feel like truth because they are sealed
off, I invite
the man with gloves to come closer.
His black cloth hood with slits as familiar to me
as the rocking boat he steps out of: a ferryman
of bodies, a liminal human who complies
in all silence;
unlike the body of any woman,
unlike the voice of the woman who tells me, tear it out,
that tree of live wire crusting with seed pearls
rooted in your blood. He climbs this tree

of eels, swings his axe
with both hands. Footgear, posture, oarlock: all one
gesture, repeating its meaning, condemned
to repeat it. After all, I am alone here,

3

in the fall of the year. In my greenhouse. The ceiling
sways, glittering with shockwaves.
Pouches of splinter hang. Nubbles of crystal
fill the small craters crushed against
the mesh skeleton. Patterns of light harlequin
my body, as if this were a dome of stained glass overhead
and its broken places, mazes of solder. The whole sky
is tender with smoke. Muted rose
suffuses the November dusk,
rising from the city like a philtre, or a promise,
and not what it is, lost darkness.

4

The doors that lead out, the French doors, are dismantled,
stored in the cellar on a broken workbench.
There's damp in the dirt floor. Some of the pumpkins
do not rot
as soon as the others; some wither: dried fibers
draw their teeth inward, bit by bit, the grin
becoming a wince.
Like the body of a woman, betrayed. Sheets of newsprint
swirl on the ground, falter
in the doorway on a skewer of wind; swept forward,

a puppet of rubbish, litter, in whose eyes I read again:
Strange chemical reactions in the old beams set
St. Luke's afire. They were not strange.
Don't call them strange, you, who depart,
and never regain,
bodies of women, living on air, all of them, on air;
as you, on air.

When I Get There

When I get there, the gate
will be littered
with leaves, lifting,

piling, in between
the pickets. All around
will be blue—the sun hot,

but far off,
and everywhere a rush
ruffling the light.

I will be so sleepy
and pleased, buffeted
by these light-laden winds,

I will lie back
down, into the leaves,
and not remember to go in.